SCAT OMNIBOOK

For Vocalists and C Instruments
Transcribed Exactly from the Original Recordings

- **3** INTRO
- **4** CONTENTS
- **272** ARTIST INDEX

Transcribed by Mark Johnson

ISBN 978-1-4803-5562-0

7777 W. BLUEMOUND RD. P.O. BOX 13819 MILWAUKEE, WI 53213

For all works contained herein:
Unauthorized copying, arranging, adapting, recording, Internet posting, public performance,
or other distribution of the printed music in this publication is an infringement of copyright.
Infringers are liable under the law.

Visit Hal Leonard Online at
www.halleonard.com

THE HISTORY OF SCAT

Scat singing is a form of jazz vocal improvisation that does not use words. Instead, the vocalist either uses nonsense syllables or imitates musical instruments.

Scat singing has its true beginnings with the 1926 Louis Armstrong recording of "Heebie Jeebies." As the story goes, during the recording session for the song, Armstrong's music fell onto the floor. To keep the recording going, he started improvising his own gibberish words over the chorus of the song, assuming it was a ruined take. After all was said and done, it was that take of "Hebbie Jeebies" that was kept, and a new genre was born.

Artists at the time who picked up on the scat trend included Cab Calloway and Duke Ellington, whose "Creole Love Call" featured Adelaide Hall doing a vocal impression of a muted trumpet. Soon, other artists joined in on the vocal craze, including Dizzy Gillespie, Eddie Jefferson, Mel Tormé, Sarah Vaughan, and a true master of the craft, Ella Fitzgerald.

It was while she was singing with Dizzy Gillespie's big band that Ella Fitzgerald started playing around with her vocals. Instead of singing lyrics, she imitated what the horns were doing. Her performance on the 1945 recording of "Flying Home" with the Vic Schoen Orchestra set a new standard for scat, much as Louis Armstrong's "Heebie Jeebies" had done years earlier.

The songs in this volume include selections by many of the classic jazz scat artists, including Ella Fitzgerald, Sarah Vaughan, Mel Tormé, and Eddie Jefferson, along with more contemporary vocalists, such as Karrin Allyson, Ann Hampton Callaway, and Roberta Gambarini.

You'll find these helpful features in this "omni" volume:
- 74 note-for-note transcriptions
- Meticulous easy-to-read notation
- Recording reference included with the song title
- No lyrics are included for the scat solos, as the spelling of syllables are too varied and numerous
- Most importantly: ANYONE can use this book, vocalists and instrumentalists alike. The solos lend themselves to vocalists wanting to learn the style, as well as horn players who wish to expand their improvising prowess.

Enjoy!

CONTENTS

6 AIR MAIL SPECIAL
Ella Fitzgerald

10 ALL BLUES
Ernestine Anderson

15 ALL GOD'S CHILLUN GOT RHYTHM
Mel Tormé

ALL OF ME
18 Ella Fitzgerald
21 Sarah Vaughan

24 BERNIE'S TUNE
Tierney Sutton

27 BILLIE'S BOUNCE (BILL'S BOUNCE)
Ella Fitzgerald

34 BLI BLIP
Ella Fitzgerald

37 BLUE LOU
Ella Fitzgerald

40 BLUE SKIES
Ella Fitzgerald

BLUESETTE
44 Ann Hampton Callaway
48 Ella Fitzgerald

56 BODY AND SOUL
Eddie Jefferson

51 CENTERPIECE
Roberta Gambarini

60 CLEMENTINE
Ella Fitzgerald

62 CRAZY RHYTHM
Ella Fitzgerald

70 DINAH
Bing Crosby

74 DIPSY DOODLE
Ella Fitzgerald

67 E AND D BLUES
Ella Fitzgerald

76 ELLA HUMS THE BLUES
Ella Fitzgerald

82 FLAT FOOT FLOOGEE
Slim Gaillard

79 FLYING HOME
Ella Fitzgerald

84 FROM THIS MOMENT ON
Roberta Gambarini

90 GEE BABY, AIN'T I GOOD TO YOU
Karrin Allyson

92 HEEBIE JEEBIES
Louis Armstrong

HONEYSUCKLE ROSE
94 Eddie Jefferson
102 Mel Tormé & Roy Eldridge

HOW HIGH THE MOON
97 Ann Hampton Callaway
108 Ella Fitzgerald

112 I AIN'T GOT NOTHIN' BUT THE BLUES
Karrin Allyson

120 I CAN'T GIVE YOU ANYTHING BUT LOVE
Sarah Vaughan

115 I GOT RHYTHM
Sheila Jordan

122 I'M IN THE MOOD FOR LOVE
King Pleasure

132 IT DON'T MEAN A THING
(IF IT AIN'T GOT THAT SWING)
Ella Fitzgerald

136 IT'S ALL RIGHT WITH ME
Connie Evingson

125 IT'S NOT FOR ME TO SAY
Tania Maria

140	JA-DA Leo Watson		215	ST. LOUIS BLUES Ella Fitzgerald
143	JUMPIN' AT THE WOODSIDE Jon Hendricks		224	SCHULIE A BOP Sarah Vaughan
148	JUST FRIENDS Mel Tormé		226	SHINY STOCKINGS Trish Hatley

JUST YOU, JUST ME
- 153 Ella Fitzgerald
- 156 Tierney Sutton

232 SING, SING, SING
Anita O'Day

236 SOME OF THESE DAYS
Bing Crosby

LINE FOR LYONS
- 162 Karrin Alllyson
- 159 Faye Claassen

229 SONG FOR MY FATHER
Dee Dee Bridgewater

LOVER, COME BACK TO ME
- 164 Roberta Gambarini
- 170 Anita O'Day

238 SQUEEZE ME
Roberta Gambarini

LULLABY OF BIRDLAND
- 173 Ann Hampton Callaway
- 176 Dianne Reeves
- 180 Mel Tormé
- 184 Sarah Vaughan

242 STOLEN MOMENTS
Mark Murphy

248 SUDDENLY IN WALKED BUD
Carmen McRae

190 MAS QUE NADA
Ella Fitzgerald

245 THERE WILL NEVER BE ANOTHER YOU
Ann Hampton Callaway

194 NATURE BOY
Kurt Elling

250 THOU SWELL
Betty Carter

OH, LADY BE GOOD!
- 187 Ann Hampton Callaway
- 198 Dianne Reeves

252 A-TISKET, A-TASKET
The Manhattan Transfer

201 OLD DEVIL MOON
Carmen McRae

256 WEST COAST BLUES
Karrin Allyson

204 ON THE SUNNY SIDE OF THE STREET
Roberta Gambarini

259 YARDBIRD SUITE
Karrin Allyson

210 PICK YOURSELF UP
Ann Hampton Callaway

262 YESTERDAYS
Dianne Reeves

222 ROCKIN' IN RHYTHM
Bunny Briggs

268 YOU'LL HAVE TO SWING IT
Ella Fitzgerald

266 ZAZ ZUH ZAZ
Cab Calloway

Air Mail Special

from *Ella Fitzgerald: Gold – Verve 951102*
Music by Benny Goodman, Jimmy Mundy and Charlie Christian

All Blues
from *Ernestine Anderson: Blues, Dues and Love News – Quest 9362-45900-2*
By Miles Davis

All God's Chillun Got Rhythm

from *Mel Tormé: It's Easy to Remember – Recall 258*

Lyrics by Gus Kahn
Music by Bronislaw Kaper and Walter Jurmann

© 1937 (Renewed) MGM CORP.
Rights Assigned to EMI CATALOGUE PARTNERSHIP
All Rights Administered by EMI Robbins Catalog Inc. (Publishing) and ALFRED MUSIC (Print)
All Rights Reserved   Used by Permission

Billie's Bounce
(Bill's Bounce)
from *Ella Fitzgerald: Bluella – Pablo 2310960*
By Charlie Parker

Blue Lou
from *Ella Fitzgerald: The Legendary Decca Recordings – GRP 648*
Words and Music by Irving Mills and Edgar Sampson

Blue ___ Lou. ___ Blue ___ Lou. ___

Her ba-by was such a pho-ny; ___ he left her blue ___ and lone-

-ly. ___ Blue ___ Lou. ___ True ___ Lou. ___

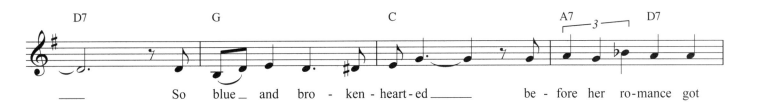
So blue ___ and bro-ken-heart-ed ___ be-fore her ro-mance got

start-ed. Cry-ing, sigh-ing ___ is all she ev-er do. ___

For-get-ting, ___ re-gret-ting ___ the love she nev-er knew. ___

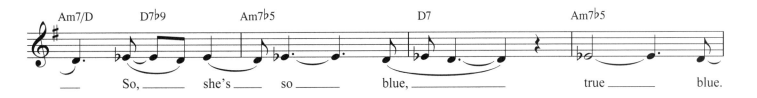
So, she's so blue, ___ true blue.

© 1961 (Renewed) EMI MILLS MUSIC INC.
All Rights Administered by EMI MILLS MUSIC INC. (Publishing) and ALFRED MUSIC (Print)
All Rights Reserved   Used by Permission

Blue Skies
from *Ella Fitzgerald Sings the Irving Berlin Songbook – Verve 5438302*
Words and Music by Irving Berlin

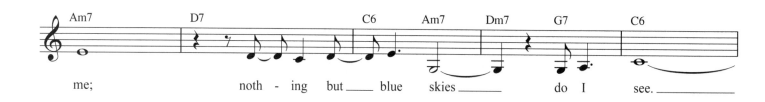

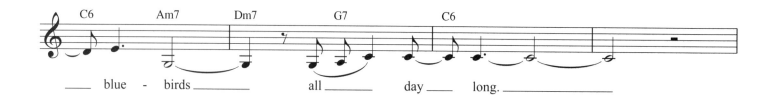

© Copyright 1927 by Irving Berlin
Copyright Renewed
International Copyright Secured   All Rights Reserved

Bluesette

from *Ann Hampton Callaway: Easy Living – Shanachie Records 5126*

Words by Norman Gimbel
Music by Jean Thielemans

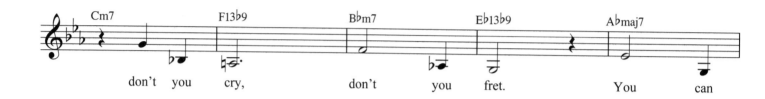

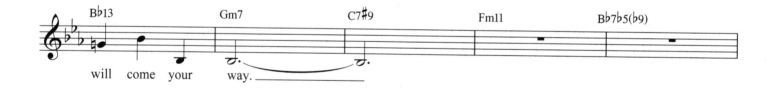

Copyright © 1963, 1964 SONGS OF UNIVERSAL, INC.
Copyright Renewed; Words Renewed 1992 by NORMAN GIMBEL for the World and Assigned to
WORDS WEST LLC (P.O. Box 15187, Beverly Hills, CA 90209 USA)
All Rights Reserved   Used by Permission

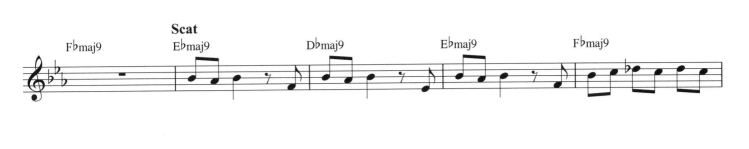

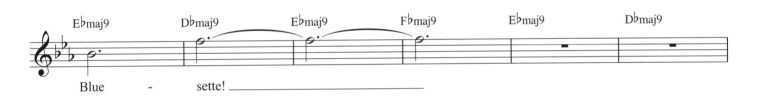
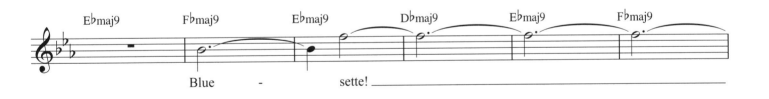
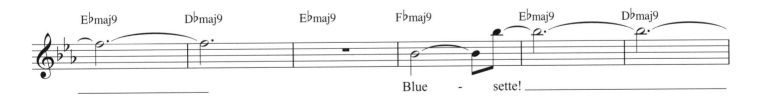
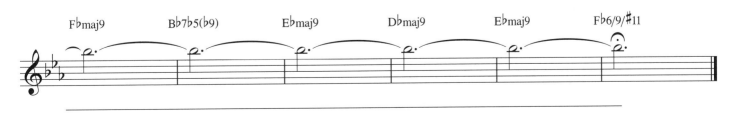

Bluesette

from *Ella Fitzgerald: Sophisticated Lady – Pablo 5310*

Words by Norman Gimbel
Music by Jean Thielemans

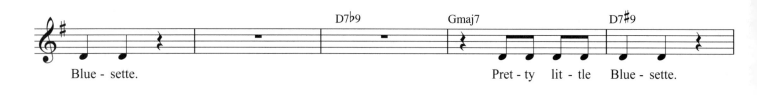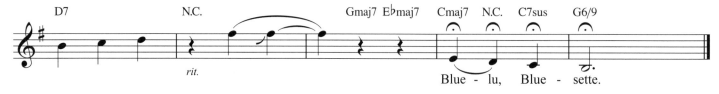

Body and Soul
from *Eddie Jefferson: Body and Soul – OJC 396*
Words by Edward Heyman, Robert Sour and Frank Eyton
Music by John Green

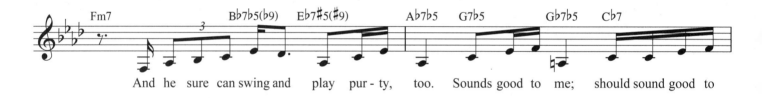

Copyright © 1930 Warner Bros. Inc.
Copyright renewed; extended term of Copyright deriving from Edward Heyman
assigned and effective January 1, 1987 to Range Road Music Inc. and Quartet Music
Extended term of Copyright deriving from John Green, Robert Sour and Frank Eyton assigned to Warner Bros. Inc. and Druropetal Music
All Rights for Quartet Music Administered by BUG Music, Inc., a BMG Chrysalis company
International Copyright Secured   All Rights Reserved
Used by Permission

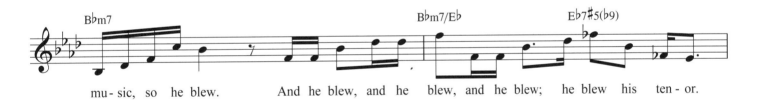

Clementine

from *Ella Fitzgerald Sings the Duke Ellington Songbook – Verve VE2-2535*
By Billy Strayhorn

Crazy Rhythm
from *Ella Fitzgerald: In Budapest – Pablo 5308*
Words by Irving Caesar
Music by Joseph Meyer and Roger Wolfe Kahn

Cra - zy Rhy - thm, here's the door - way;
Here is where we have a show - down;

I'll go my way, you go your way. Cra - zy Rhy - thm,
I'm too high if you're the low down. Cra - zy Rhy - thm,

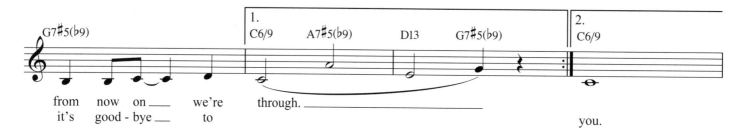

from now on we're through.
it's good - bye to you.

I know that when a high - brow meets a low - brow walk-

-ing a - long Broad - way, soon a high - brow, he has no brow. Ain't

it a shame! And you're to blame! What's the use of

Pro - hi - bi - tion? You pro - duce the same con - di - tion.

Copyright © 1928 (Renewed) Larry Spier Music LLC, Irving Caesar Music and WB Music Corp.
All Rights on behalf of Irving Caesar Music Administered by WB Music Corp.
International Copyright Secured   All Rights Reserved

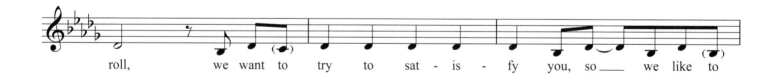

Dinah

from *Bing Crosby: 16 Most Requested Songs – Columbia/Legacy CK-48974*

Words by Sam M. Lewis and Joe Young
Music by Harry Akst

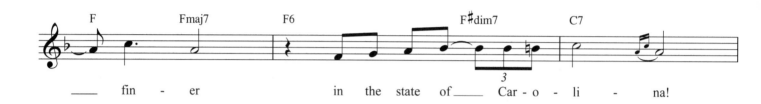

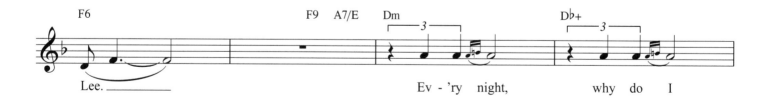

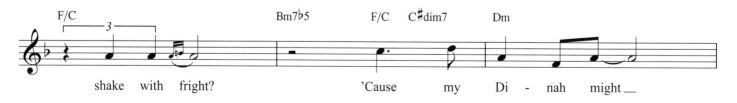

© 1925 MILLS MUSIC, INC.
© Renewed MORLEY MUSIC CO., B & G AKST PUBLISHING CO. and MILLS MUSIC, INC.
Harry Akst Reversionary Interest Controlled by BOURNE CO. (ASCAP)
All Rights Reserved

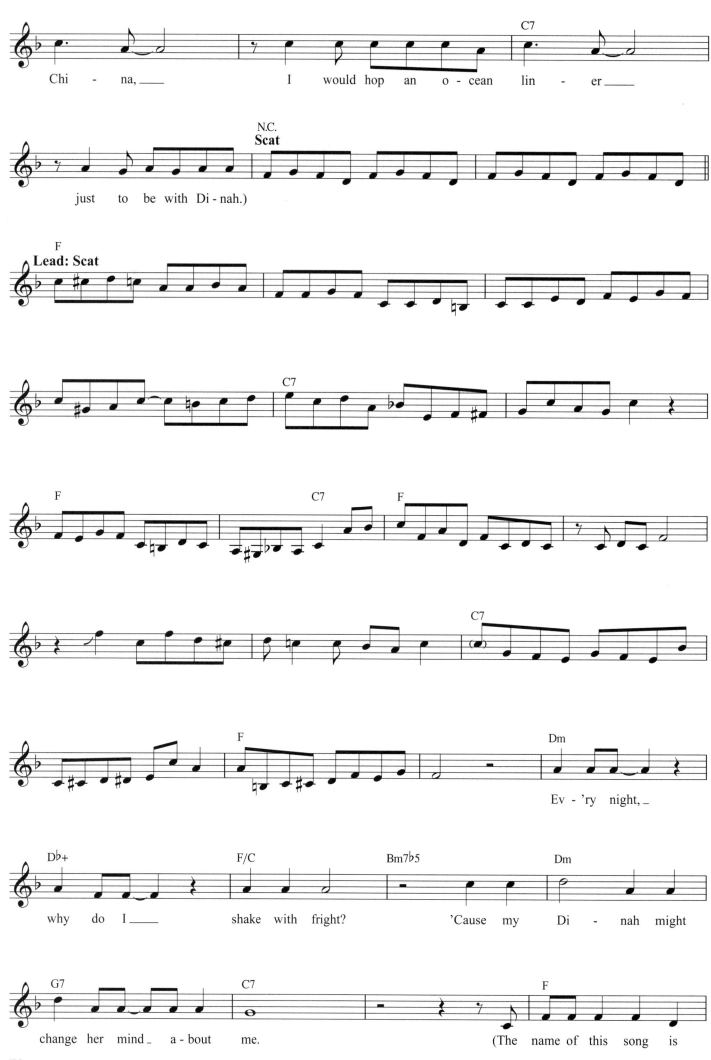

Dipsy Doodle
from *Ella Fitzgerald: The Early Years Pt. 1 – GRP 26182*
By Larry Clinton

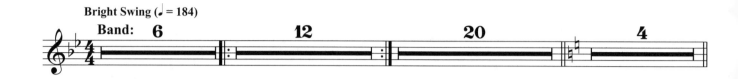

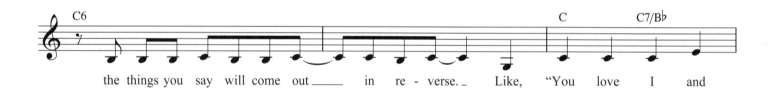

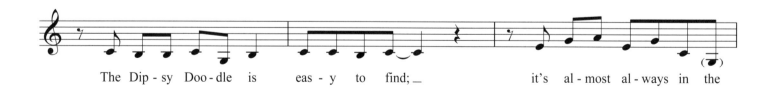

Copyright © 1964 (Renewed), 1979 Dulcet Music Company
All Rights Administered by The Songwriters Guild Of America
All Rights Reserved   Used by Permission

Ella Hums the Blues

from *Ella Fitzgerald: Songs from Pete Kelly's Blues – Decca DL 8166*
Words by Sammy Cahn
Music by Ray Heindorf

© 1955 (Renewed) MARK VII LTD.
All Rights Administered by WB MUSIC CORP.
All Rights Reserved   Used by Permission

Flying Home

from *Ella Fitzgerald: Gold – Verve B951102*

Music by Benny Goodman and Lionel Hampton
Lyric by Sid Robin

Flat Foot Floogee
from *Slim Gaillard: Cement Mixer – Proper 1347*
Words and Music by Slim Gaillard, Slam Stewart and Bud Green

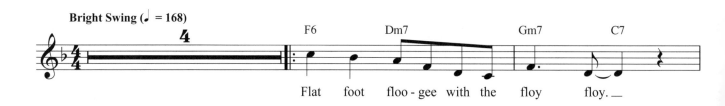
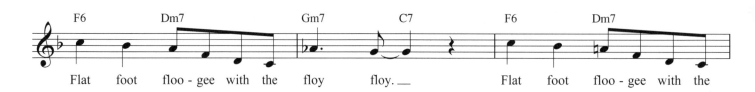
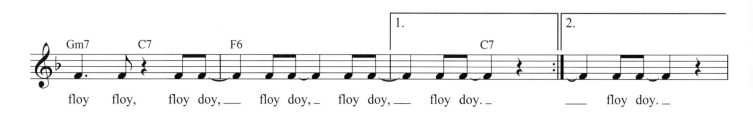

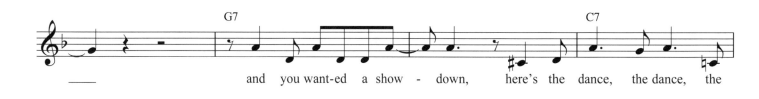

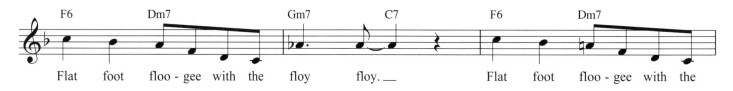

Copyright © 1938 (Renewed) by Jewel Music Publishing Co., Inc. (ASCAP), Holliday Publications (ASCAP)
and O'Vouti Publishing (ASCAP) in the United States
International Copyright Secured   All Rights Reserved
Used by Permission

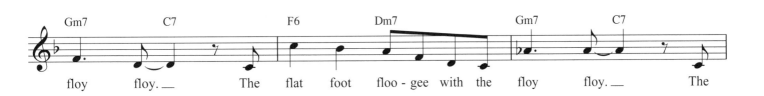
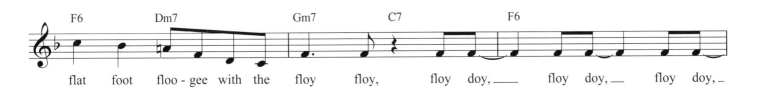
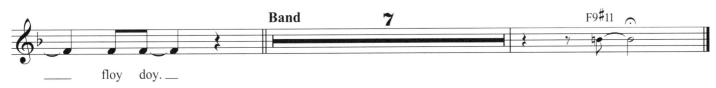

Heebie Jeebies

from *Louis Armstrong: The Best of the Hot Five and Hot Seven Recordings – Sony 5055*

By Boyd Atkins

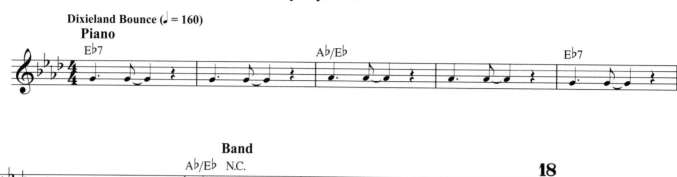

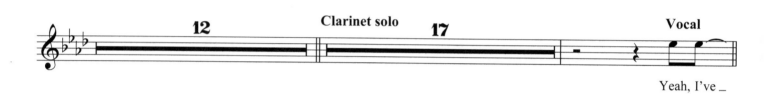

Yeah, I've _

_ got the Hee-bie, I mean the Jee-bies. Talk-in' a-bout

the dance, the Hee-bie Jee-bies. Do, be - cause they're boys, _

'cause it _ brings a lit-tle bit o' joy. Say, don't you know it?

You don't know how? Don't be blue; come on, we'll teach you.

Come on, _ and do that dance _ they call the Hee-bie Jee-bies dance. _

Copyright © 1926 UNIVERSAL MUSIC CORP.
Copyright Renewed
All Rights Reserved   Used by Permission

Honeysuckle Rose

from *Eddie Jefferson: The Jazz Singer – Evidence 22062*

Words by Andy Razaf
Music by Thomas "Fats" Waller

Copyright © 1929 by Chappell & Co., Inc. and Razaf Music
Copyright Renewed
All Rights for Razaf Music Administered by BMG Rights Management (US) LLC
International Copyright Secured   All Rights Reserved

Honeysuckle Rose

from *Roy Eldridge and Mel Tormé:*
1947 WNEW Saturday Night Swing Session – Everest FS 231
Words by Andy Razaf
Music by Thomas "Fats" Waller

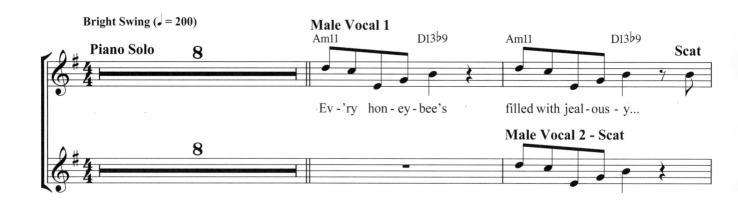

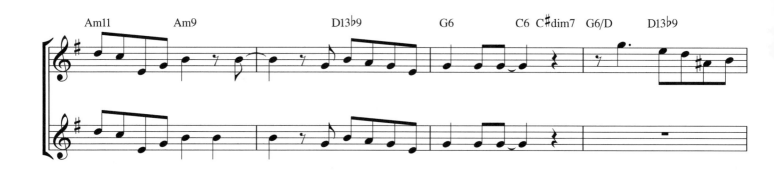

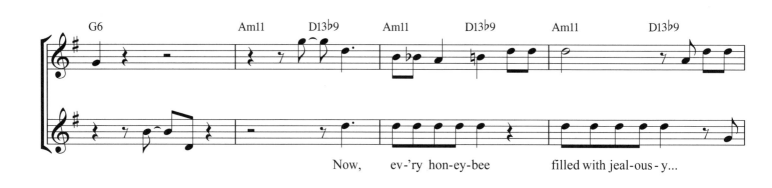

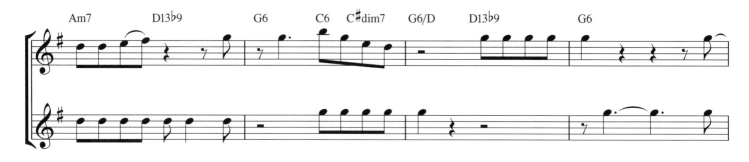

Copyright © 1929 by Chappell & Co., Inc. and Razaf Music
Copyright Renewed
All Rights for Razaf Music Administered by BMG Rights Management (US) LLC
International Copyright Secured   All Rights Reserved

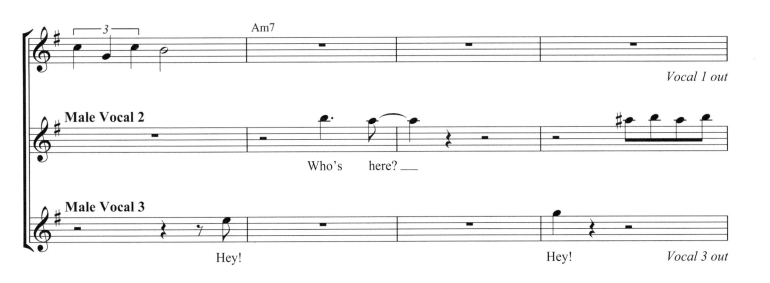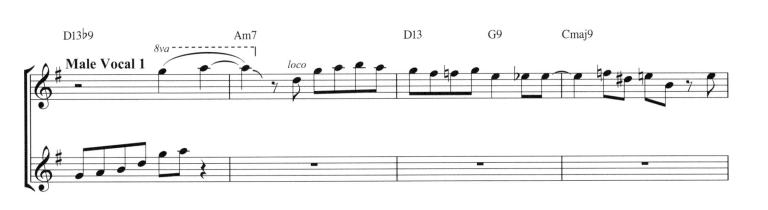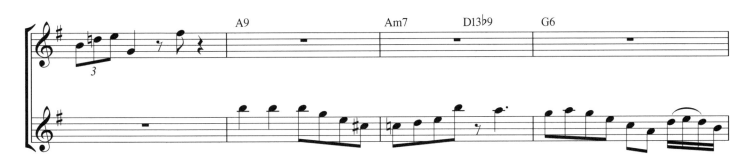

How High the Moon

from *Ella Fitzgerald: Lullabies of Birdland* – Verve 1724765

Lyrics by Nancy Hamilton
Music by Morgan Lewis

I Ain't Got Nothin' But the Blues

from *Karrin Allyson: Daydream – Concord 4773*

Words by Don George
Music by Duke Ellington

Copyright © 1937, 1944 Sony/ATV Music Publishing LLC, Ricki Music Company and True Blue Music Publishing Company
Copyright Renewed
All Rights on behalf of Sony/ATV Music Publishing LLC Administered by
Sony/ATV Music Publishing LLC, 424 Church Street, Suite 1200, Nashville, TN 37219
All Rights on behalf of Ricki Music Company Administered by WB Music Corp.
All Rights on behalf of True Blue Music Publishing Company in the U.S. Administered by Spirit Two Music, Inc.
International Copyright Secured   All Rights Reserved

I'm in the Mood for Love
from *King Pleasure: Moody's Mood for Love – Collectables 5197*
Words and Music by Jimmy McHugh and Dorothy Fields

It's Not for Me to Say

from *Tania Maria: The Beat of Brazil – View Video 72034*

Words by Al Stillman
Music by Robert Allen

Ja-Da

from *Leo Watson: Anthology of Scat Singing, Vol. 3 – Masters of Jazz 803*

Words and Music by Bob Carleton

Jumpin' at the Woodside

from *Jon Hendricks and Friends: Freddie Freeloader – Sony 53487*

Music by Count Basie
Words by Jon Hendricks

Just Friends

from *Mel Tormé: Rob McConnell and the Boss Brass – Concord CCD 4306*

Lyrics by Sam M. Lewis
Music by John Klenner

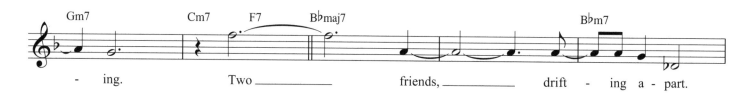

© 1931 (Renewed) METRO-GOLDWYN-MAYER, INC.
All Rights Controlled by EMI ROBBINS CATALOG INC. (Publishing) and ALFRED MUSIC (Print)
All Rights Reserved Used by Permission

Line for Lyons

from *Fay Claassen Sings Two Portraits of Chet Baker – Jazz N' Pulz 497*
By Gerry Mulligan

Line for Lyons

from *Karrin Allyson: I Didn't Know About You – Concord Jazz 4543*
By Gerry Mulligan

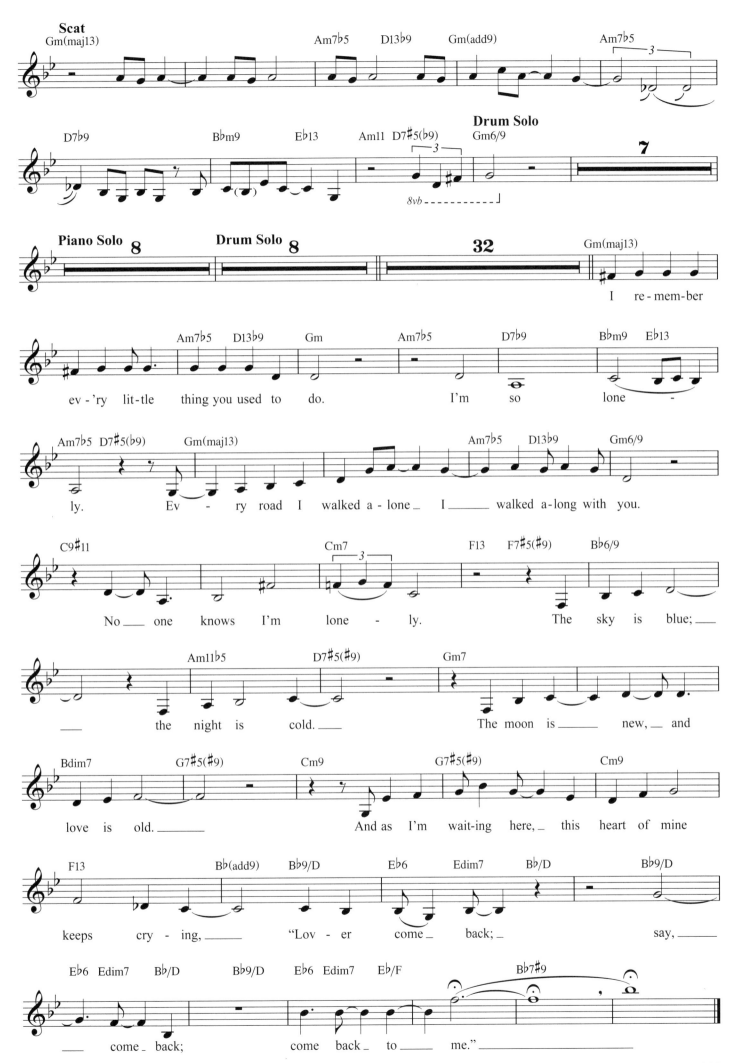

Lullaby of Birdland

from *Ann Hampton Callaway: To Ella with Love – Sindrome 71577689332*

Words by George David Weiss
Music by George Shearing

© 1952, 1954 (Renewed 1980, 1982) EMI Longitude Music and Abilene Music LLC
All Rights for Abilene Music LLC Administered Worldwide by Imagem Music LLC
All Rights Reserved   International Copyright Secured   Used by Permission

Oh, Lady Be Good!
from *Ann Hampton Callaway: To Ella with Love – Sindrome 71577689332*
Music and Lyrics by George Gershwin and Ira Gershwin

Oh, Lady Be Good!
from *Dianne Reeves: We All Love Ella – Verve 8833*
Music and Lyrics by George Gershwin and Ira Gershwin

On the Sunny Side of the Street

from *Roberta Gambarini: Easy to Love – New Forward Music Inc. 1122*

Lyric by Dorothy Fields
Music by Jimmy McHugh

Pick Yourself Up

from *Ann Hampton Callaway: Signature – Shanachie 5127*

Words by Dorothy Fields
Music by Jerome Kern

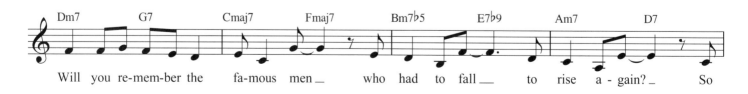

St. Louis Blues

from *Ella Fitzgerald: Twelve Nights in Hollywood – Hip-O Select 2704402*
Words and Music by W.C. Handy

Copyright © 2015 by HAL LEONARD CORPORATION
International Copyright Secured   All Rights Reserved

Schulie A Bop

from *Sarah Vaughan's Finest Hour – Verve 5435972*
Words and Music by Sarah Vaughan and George Treadwell

Song for My Father

from *Dee Dee Bridgewater: Love and Peace – Verve/Polygram 5274702*

Words and Music by Horace Silver

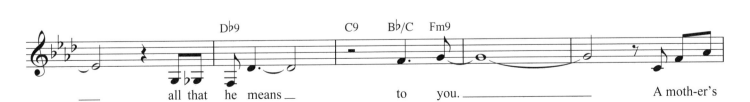

Sing, Sing, Sing

from *Anita O'Day Sings the Winners – Verve AA8379392*

Words and Music by Louis Prima

Squeeze Me

from *Roberta Gambarini: You Are There – Emarcy 1737067*
Words and Music by Clarence Williams and Thomas "Fats" Waller

There Will Never Be Another You

from *Ann Hampton Callaway: Bring Back Romance – DRG 91417*

Lyric by Mack Gordon
Music by Harry Warren

This is our last dance to-geth-er;

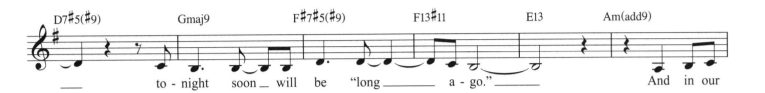
to-night soon will be "long a-go." And in our

mo-ment of part-ing, this is all I want you to

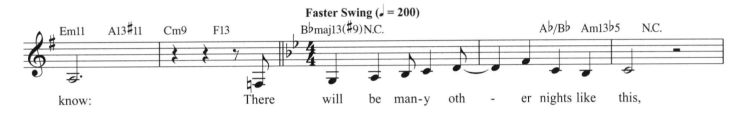
know: There will be man-y oth-er nights like this,

and I'll be stand-ing here with some-one new.

There will be oth-er songs to sing, an-oth-er fall, an-

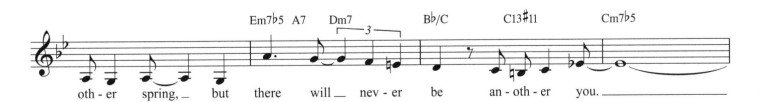
oth-er spring, but there will nev-er be an-oth-er you.

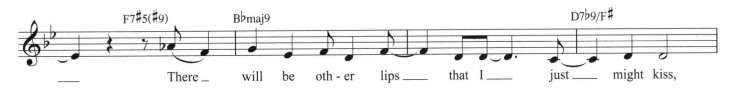
There will be oth-er lips that I just might kiss,

© 1942 (Renewed) MORLEY MUSIC CO., FOUR JAYS MUSIC PUBLISHING and MATTSAM MUSIC
All Rights Reserved

Thou Swell

from *Meet Betty Carter and Ray Bryant – Epic 3202*

Words by Lorenz Hart
Music by Richard Rodgers

A-Tisket, A-Tasket

from *The Manhattan Transfer: Couldn't Be Hotter – Telarc 83586*

Words and Music by Ella Fitzgerald and Van Alexander

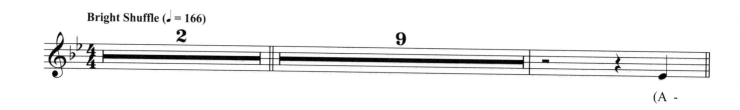

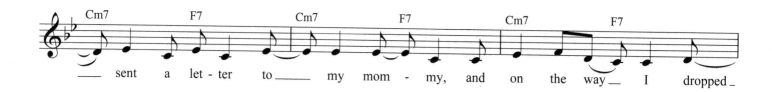

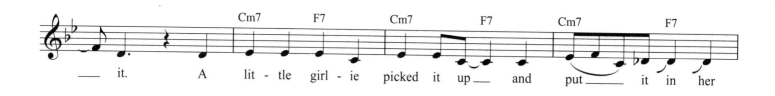

© 1938 (Renewed) EMI ROBBINS CATALOG INC.
All Rights Administered by EMI ROBBINS CATALOG INC. (Publishing) and ALFRED MUSIC (Print)
All Rights Reserved Used by Permission

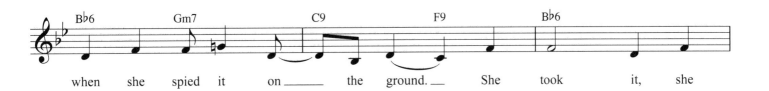

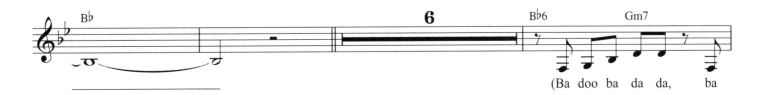
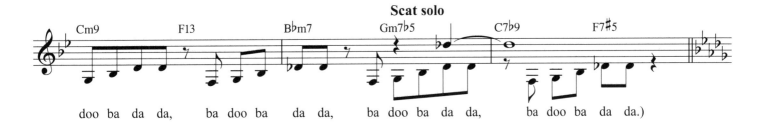

West Coast Blues

from *Karrin Allyson: In Blue* – Concord 2106CCJ
Music by John L. (Wes) Montgomery
Lyrics by Sascha Burland

Zaz Zuh Zaz

from *Cab Calloway: On Film 1934-1950 – Flyright 944*
Words and Music by Cab Calloway and Harry A. White

ARTIST INDEX

KARRIN ALLYSON
90 Gee Baby, Ain't I Good to You
112 I Ain't Got Nothin' but the Blues
162 Line for Lyons
256 West Coast Blues
259 Yardbird Suite

ERNESTINE ANDERSON
10 All Blues

LOUIS ARMSTRONG
92 Heebie Jeebies

DEE DEE BRIDGEWATER
229 Song for My Father

BUNNY BRIGGS
222 Rockin' in Rhythm

ANN HAMPTON CALLAWAY
44 Bluesette
97 How High the Moon
173 Lullaby of Birdland
187 Oh, Lady Be Good!
210 Pick Yourself Up
245 There Will Never Be Another You

CAB CALLOWAY
266 Zaz Zuh Zaz

BETTY CARTER
250 Thou Swell

FAYE CLAASSEN
159 Line for Lyons

BING CROSBY
70 Dinah
236 Some of These Days

KURT ELLING
194 Nature Boy

CONNIE EVINGSON
136 It's All Right with Me

ELLA FITZGERALD
6 Air Mail Special
18 All of Me
27 Billie's Bounce
34 Bli Blip
37 Blue Lou
40 Blue Skies
48 Bluesette
60 Clementine
62 Crazy Rhythm
74 The Dipsy Doodle
67 E and D Blues
76 Ella Hums the Blues
79 Flying Home
108 How High the Moon
132 It Don't Mean a Thing
153 Just You, Just Me
190 Mas Que Nada
215 St. Louis Blues
268 You'll Have to Swing It

SLIM GAILLARD
82 Flat Foot Floogie

ROBERTA GAMBARINI
51 Centerpiece
84 From This Moment On
164 Lover, Come Back to Me
204 On the Sunny Side of the Street
238 Squeeze Me

TRISH HATLEY
226 Shiny Stockings

JON HENDRICKS
143 Jumpin' at the Woodside

EDDIE JEFFERSON
56 Body and Soul
94 Honeysuckle Rose

SHEILA JORDAN
115 I Got Rhythm

THE MANHATTAN TRANSFER
252 A-Tisket, A-Tasket

TANIA MARIA
125 It's Not for Me to Say

CARMEN McRAE
201 Old Devil Moon
248 Suddenly In Walked Bud

MARK MURPHY
242 Stolen Moments

ANITA O'DAY
170 Lover, Come Back to Me
232 Sing, Sing, Sing

KING PLEASURE
122 I'm in the Mood for Love

DIANNE REEVES
176 Lullaby of Birdland
198 Oh, Lady Be Good!
262 Yesterdays

TIERNEY SUTTON
24 Bernie's Tune
156 Just You, Just Me

MEL TORMÉ
15 All God's Chillun Got Rhythm
102 Honeysuckle Rose
    (w/Roy Eldridge)
148 Just Friends
180 Lullaby of Birdland

SARAH VAUGHAN
21 All of Me
120 I Can't Give You Anything
    But Love
184 Lullaby of Birdland
224 Schulie a Bop

LEO WATSON
140 Ja-Da